365

WISDOM

Whispers

FOR THE SOUL

AMANDA NABORS

HOV
PUBLISHING

365 Wisdom Whispers For The Soul

Copyright ©2024 by Amanda Nabors

Unless otherwise noted, Scriptures are taken from The King James Version. Copyright © 1982 by Thomas Nelson, Inc. Used by permission. All rights reserved.

HOV Publishing is a division of HOV, LLC.
Bridgeport, CT 06605
Email: hopeofvision@gmail.com
www.hovpub.com
www.90daybookcreation.com

Cover Design and Layout: HOV Designs
Editor: HOV Publishing editing team

Contact the Author:
Amanda Nabors
hisjoy@bellsouth.net

For further information regarding special discounts on bulk purchases, please contact: Amanda Nabors at hisjoy@bellsouth.net.

ISBN Paperback: 978-1-955107-41-9
ISBN eBook: 978-1-955107-40-2

Printed in the United States of America

- ENDORSEMENTS -

If you desire to maximize your life to the apex level of effectiveness, then the wisdom in 365 Wisdom Whispers For The Soul is for you. From her intimate covenant daily relationship with God, Minister Amanda outlines a daily strategy to elevate your faith walk, nourish your soul's maturity, and encourage and enlighten you with the daily bread of wisdom from God's voice. In addition, you will find that when you apply these pertinent truths as found in the pages of this book, spiritual wisdom will provide meaningful resources beyond what money can buy to resource your life to fulfill your purpose.

Join me in encouraging and supporting my spiritual granddaughter as she continues to be a "His-story maker, mover, and shaker," representing the Kingdom of God's influence.

Apostolic Bishop, Darryl Jackson
Founder of Church of The Firstborn Ministries, Inc., and Apostolic Covenant Family of Ministries.

- DEDICATION -

I want to dedicate this book to my family, church family, friends, my spiritual fathers and mothers, Pastor Joe and Shawneice Brock, Apostle Darryl Jackson and Pastor Beverly Jackson, and most of all, to my Heavenly Father, who always graciously showers me with an abundance of goodness and mercy. Every day, He crowns me with lovingkindness and sweetly whispers many treasures to my heart, timely words ready to be penned, spoken, and shared.

Abba Father, thank You for giving Your daughter a tongue as the pen of a ready writer, words of wisdom, love, truth, understanding, revelation, hope, peace, and comfort. My sincere prayer is for all who read these words of daily encouragement, affirmations, and truths to hear Your voice speak generously to their souls, and as they partake, they will be still and know You are perfecting all things that concern them. Peace, and
Grace Be Multiplied.

- SCRIPTURES -

Finally, brethren, whatsoever things are true, whatsoever things *are* honest, whatsoever things *are* Just, whatsoever things *are* Pure, whatsoever things *are* lovely, whatsoever things *are* of good report; if there be any virtue, and if *there be* any praise, think on these things. ~ Philippians 4:8

My heart is inditing a good matter: speaking of the things which I have made touching my King: My tongue is the pen of a ready writer.

~ Psalm 45:1

Speak Lord, and I shall hear.

- FOREWORD -

It is our absolute joy to witness this truly wonderful prophetic book of daily wisdom and prophetic inspiration. Amanda, an Ordained Minister, has once again written a book from which you can receive spiritual life and divine nuggets for each day of the year. You will find reflection, clarity of thought, and encouragement to help uplift your souls. We celebrate another accomplishment in obedience.

Proverbs 4:7, "Wisdom is the principal thing; therefore get wisdom: And with all thy getting get understanding."

Minister Amanda's writings contain wisdom and understanding to strengthen one's soulish stamina and walk with the Lord.

Proverbs 24:3-4, "Through wisdom is an house builded; And by understanding it is established: And by knowledge shall the chambers be filled With all precious and pleasant riches."

This passage reflects that our Father, through wisdom and understanding by knowledge, fortifies us in our living. In this world, there are innumerable trains of thought. Safeguarding your heart's meditation using plain-spoken insights can keep you focused on soulish and spiritual refinement. You don't want to miss out on this impartation.

Blessings and Live,
Pastors Joe & Shawn Brock
Cutting Edge Ministries Church
Cottondale, Alabama

*A friend asked me if I play cards, I told him not since I was...Fooled by a **Joker**, **Heart**-broken, hit by a **Club**, jilted out of a **Diamond** and called a **Spade**! Now this **Queen** has a **King** and He is her **ACE**…Jesus!*

~ Amanda Nabors

- INTRODUCTION -

"365 Wisdom Whispers For The Soul" by Amanda Nabors is an enriching collection of daily inspirations designed to offer guidance, comfort, and a deeper understanding of life's journey. Each day of the year is graced with a unique quote or saying, thoughtfully curated to ignite reflection and foster personal growth.

As you turn the pages of this book, you will be greeted with words that resonate with the challenges and joys of everyday life. Amanda has carefully selected each piece of wisdom, drawing from diverse sources and cultures, ensuring that every reader finds a connection. Whether you're seeking motivation, contemplation, or a moment of peace on a busy day, these sayings act as gentle whispers to the soul, encouraging you to pause and ponder.

"365 Wisdom Whispers For The Soul" is more than just a book of quotes; it's a daily companion on your journey towards self-discovery and inner peace. It serves as a reminder of the beauty and truth hidden in the ordinary, inviting you to embrace life's complexities with an open heart and a curious mind. Each entry is an opportunity to reflect on life's lessons and to find joy and wisdom in the simplicity of the day-to-day.

This book is a treasure trove of insights, ideal for morning meditations, evening reflections, or quick midday inspiration. It's perfect for anyone looking to infuse their day with a dose of mindful wisdom and soulful introspection. Let "365 Wisdom Whispers For The Soul" guide you through the year, one empowering and enlightening whisper at a time.

365
WISDOM
Whispers
FOR THE SOUL

365 WISDOM WHISPER ~ 1

"
Sometimes, the baggage of life can be too weighty to carry, and those who are close to you may try to carry it as their own.

---

365 WISDOM WHISPER ~ 2

"
Tomorrow is not promised, but our destiny with Christ is!

---

365 WISDOM WHISPER ~ 3

"
God can use the things of this world to reveal the excellency of His wisdom.

365 WISDOM WHISPER ~ 4

" To show humility in winning can speak louder than entitlement.

---

365 WISDOM WHISPER ~ 5

" Sometimes, we enter into relationships numb, looking for others to be our anesthetic, which can prove to be deadly.

---

365 WISDOM WHISPER ~ 6

" When our back is against the wall, our eyes can focus on what's ahead and move forward.

365 WISDOM WHISPER ~ 7

"
Don't let the words of others devalue you. What we choose to believe is what we become.

---

365 WISDOM WHISPER ~ 8

"
The games people play can become our own when we abide by their rules.

---

365 WISDOM WHISPER ~ 9

"
Our life is an open book. We don't know who is reading it from cover to cover.

365 WISDOM WHISPER ~ 10

" No one's life consists of blank pages. Sometimes, what we fail to see is very obvious to others.

---

365 WISDOM WHISPER ~ 11

" Sometimes, a rude awakening is the very eye-opener that we need to see the Light.

---

365 WISDOM WHISPER ~ 12

" If you don't want to walk a mile in my shoes, that's okay. Just stay off my toes!

365 WISDOM WHISPER ~ 13

"
Narcissists can't see themselves because they are blinded by pride.

---

365 WISDOM WHISPER ~ 14

"
Sometimes, those who keep silent say more than those who talk.

---

365 WISDOM WHISPER ~ 15

"
Other's trash can become our treasure, and sometimes, what we treasure, we can trash.

365 WISDOM WHISPER ~ 16

" Purpose cannot be earned or bought; it was given.

_____

365 WISDOM WHISPER ~ 17

" How you permit others to treat you will not cease until you decide not to allow it.

_____

365 WISDOM WHISPER ~ 18

" A setback for some of us can be a reset. Calibration!

365 WISDOM WHISPER ~ 19

" Yes, it's possible to be the change we want to see in others, no matter what they show us.

---

365 WISDOM WHISPER ~ 20

" To be an instrument of change is not always about what we say. It is about what we do.

---

365 WISDOM WHISPER ~ 21

" A challenge for some may seem like defeat, but for others, it's an opportunity.

365 WISDOM WHISPER ~ 22

" A lie may seem easy to tell, but so is the truth when we are ready to be transparent.

---

365 WISDOM WHISPER ~ 23

" Our legacy is much more than material possessions. Our character, conduct, and choices are valuable.

---

365 WISDOM WHISPER ~ 24

" My story might not be your story, but if you take the time to read it, the similarities might leave you speechless.

365 WISDOM WHISPER ~ 25

"
Our life is like a movie screen, and our audience is comprised of those who know us best.

---

365 WISDOM WHISPER ~ 26

"
We can eat the words of fools and still be hungry.

---

365 WISDOM WHISPER ~ 27

"
Believing in the impossible can change our reality.

365 WISDOM WHISPER ~ 28

" If we receive respect only from our riches, in poverty, it can be lost.

---

365 WISDOM WHISPER ~ 29

" A photograph is only a picture; as life happens, it becomes a memory.

---

365 WISDOM WHISPER ~ 30

" Others sometimes bring us trash because they perceive us as their trash can. Keep a lid on it; I promise they will have to take it elsewhere.

365 WISDOM WHISPER ~ 31

" Hate has no color, only a voice.

---

365 WISDOM WHISPER ~ 32

" A gun in the hand of a fool can be deadly, and the word from the mouth of the wise can save your soul.

---

365 WISDOM WHISPER ~ 33

" Roadblocks are not necessarily stumbling blocks; it's time to make that detour.

365 WISDOM WHISPER ~ 34

"
Salt and sweet are totally opposite, but they can complement each other very well.

---

365 WISDOM WHISPER ~ 35

"
A heart that retreats to self-pity can impede healing.

---

365 WISDOM WHISPER ~ 36

"
It is time to practice what we preach and preach what we practice.

365 WISDOM WHISPER ~ 37

"
The pain of our past can hinder us only when we believe that it can.

---

365 WISDOM WHISPER ~ 38

"
Words can bring offense, but it is up to me to embrace it!

---

365 WISDOM WHISPER ~ 39

"
Our Father owns everything, even our enemies who are against us.

365 WISDOM WHISPER ~ 40

"
    The moment you accept that you are defeated, you are, but the moment you declare you are a winner, you can!

_____

365 WISDOM WHISPER ~ 41

"
    If there is a thin line between love and hate, was it ever love?

_____

365 WISDOM WHISPER ~ 42

"
    To be intelligent does not mean we know the truth.

365 WISDOM WHISPER ~ 43

"
Love is understood in all languages!

---

365 WISDOM WHISPER ~ 44

"
Love is mandatory. Hate is your choice.

---

365 WISDOM WHISPER ~ 45

"
I was not made for your amusement. I was made for His pleasure.

365 WISDOM WHISPER ~ 46

" Humility might not always be seen in those who weep, but it is truly seen in those who serve.

---

365 WISDOM WHISPER ~ 47

" A bridge is not built to divide but to carry. God has called the Church to be a bridge. Who are you carrying?

---

365 WISDOM WHISPER ~ 48

" Our time on this earth is short in comparison to eternity. Now, I have come to realize that eternity is in me!

365 WISDOM WHISPER ~ 49

"	Sometimes, it's hard for people to believe in you when they don't believe in themselves.

---

365 WISDOM WHISPER ~ 50

"	Don't despise small beginnings; they are stepping stones to your destiny.

---

365 WISDOM WHISPER ~ 51

"	The school of hard knocks teaches us to knock louder. If it's your door, it shall open!

365 WISDOM WHISPER ~ 52

"
Our past doesn't determine we are damaged goods. What we permit, we accept.

---

365 WISDOM WHISPER ~ 53

"
When we fall, we can rise. Be careful how you rise. Pride can be your downfall.

---

365 WISDOM WHISPER ~ 54

"
Every grey strand is a gift from God. We should know that because He counts them.

365 WISDOM WHISPER ~ 55

"
Those who are quick to judge are never ready to receive it.

---

365 WISDOM WHISPER ~ 56

"
The words of a bully can be sharp. They are wounded and seek to inflict their pain on others.

---

365 WISDOM WHISPER ~ 57

"
There is a jungle out there waiting on the Lion in you!

365 WISDOM WHISPER ~ 58

" You can shoot the messenger, but the truth cannot die.

---

365 WISDOM WHISPER ~ 59

" If God orders our steps, why should we make other's footsteps our own?

---

365 WISDOM WHISPER ~ 60

" Some people may see you as blank pages but don't fret. You are His story, and you are the bestseller of all time!

365 WISDOM WHISPER ~ 61

" Preaching to the choir isn't a bad thing. Sometimes, they need to hear a new song to birth new life!

---

365 WISDOM WHISPER ~ 62

" Deception is not easy to detect. If it were, it wouldn't be deception.

---

365 WISDOM WHISPER ~ 63

" Our God is always in the mood for love. HE IS LOVE!

365 WISDOM WHISPER ~ 64

" If I told you that you hurt my feelings, I just gave you the power to do it again.

---

365 WISDOM WHISPER ~ 65

" To grow old gracefully is to see yourself as God sees you and live!

---

365 WISDOM WHISPER ~ 66

" The facts of life may not be the truth, especially if they're scripted.

365 WISDOM WHISPER ~ 67

" Love has no boundaries, but hate is limited because it divides.

---

365 WISDOM WHISPER ~ 68

" The apple that falls from the tree is its fruit. I am the apple of His eye!

---

365 WISDOM WHISPER ~ 69

" Because we stumble, it doesn't mean we will fall.

365 WISDOM WHISPER ~ 70

" Justice has a voice, even if we are too deaf to hear it.

---

365 WISDOM WHISPER ~ 71

" A merry heart is good, like medicine. Take a dose as often as you can. It's prescribed!

---

365 WISDOM WHISPER ~ 72

" We never get too old to learn because we are constantly being tested.

365 WISDOM WHISPER ~ 73

" A heart that can give forgiveness is a heart that can receive it.

---

365 WISDOM WHISPER ~ 74

" Hate can blind our eyes and deafen our ears if we allow it.

---

365 WISDOM WHISPER ~ 75

" The living can raise the dead, but the dead can't raise the living.

365 WISDOM WHISPER ~ 76

"
Don't worry about what others think about you. It is only their thoughts until you make them your own.

---

365 WISDOM WHISPER ~ 77

"
When we treat others like we want to be treated, we don't have to walk in their shoes because we see them as we see ourselves.

---

365 WISDOM WHISPER ~ 78

"
Complacency is like a flat tire; it can hinder mobility.

365 WISDOM WHISPER ~ 79

"
    Sometimes, people rent space in our heads because we allow them to be tenants. Time to evacuate your premises!

_____

365 WISDOM WHISPER ~ 80

"
    Love's duty is seen in love's purpose.

_____

365 WISDOM WHISPER ~ 81

"
    When dreams of equality become a united reality, healing can begin.

365 WISDOM WHISPER ~ 82

" Jealousy and envy are related, and hatred is definitely a part of the family.

---

365 WISDOM WHISPER ~ 83

" Adversity is not seen as the spice of life. But it is a good ingredient for character building.

---

365 WISDOM WHISPER ~ 84

" People might not know your worth, but that's okay. More than likely, they don't know their own.

365 WISDOM WHISPER ~ 85

"
Be careful what you wish upon others; it might be a command reality for yourself.

---

365 WISDOM WHISPER ~ 86

"
If judgments are welcomed, soon they will occupy.

---

365 WISDOM WHISPER ~ 87

"
When we see others through the eyes of mistrust, the eyes that look upon us might see the same.

365 WISDOM WHISPER ~ 88

"
Those who demand honor may only receive appeasement.

---

365 WISDOM WHISPER ~ 89

"
If you think you know me by what you see on the outside, that's on you. If I let you mistreat me for how you see me, that's on me.

---

365 WISDOM WHISPER ~ 90

"
Mistakes are only MISS-takes; you can always try again.

365 WISDOM WHISPER ~ 91

" Humble pies can't be bought or sold.
Nobody wants them.

---

365 WISDOM WHISPER ~ 92

" Motivating others may come easy.
Motivating ourselves may involve practicing
what we preach.

---

365 WISDOM WHISPER ~ 93

" Sometimes, when we lose ourselves in
others, it may be hard to find ourselves
again.

365 WISDOM WHISPER ~ 94

" Beauty may fade, but the beauty of a loving heart is unforgettable.

---

365 WISDOM WHISPER ~ 95

" Don't be afraid to let others see the real you. It might be just what they need to reveal who they are.

---

365 WISDOM WHISPER ~ 96

" When we see people as sin, what do we see when we look in the mirror?

365 WISDOM WHISPER ~ 97

"
    Every midnight faces the light of dawn, and each day, it has to surrender!

---

365 WISDOM WHISPER ~ 98

"
    If we don't believe in ourselves, how can we convince others?

---

365 WISDOM WHISPER ~ 99

"
    Warning! Murmuring and complaining can be highly contagious. Avoid those who are infectious.

365 WISDOM WHISPER ~ 100

" It is good to love the skin that you are in; you are the only one who has it.

---

365 WISDOM WHISPER ~ 101

" Some people love to rehearse other people's mistakes. Maybe it's because they don't make any.

---

365 WISDOM WHISPER ~ 102

" I am not a copy of someone else. I am the Original!

365 WISDOM WHISPER ~ 103

" Sometimes, we see what others want us to see until we wake up and see the truth.

---

365 WISDOM WHISPER ~ 104

" To think outside the box is to use the part of our brain that is ready to be put to work.

---

365 WISDOM WHISPER ~ 105

" An uncertain heart can lead to fear, but a trusting heart can produce faith.

365 WISDOM WHISPER ~ 106

"
    If we are out of touch with reality, living in a world of make-believe is easy.

---

365 WISDOM WHISPER ~ 107

"
    The spirit of prejudice walks in pride. The spirit of humility walks in honor.

---

365 WISDOM WHISPER ~ 108

"
    Eyes that only see darkness are eyes that are void of light!

365 WISDOM WHISPER ~ 109

" The doors of opportunity are always available. Most of the time, we use the wrong keys.

---

365 WISDOM WHISPER ~ 110

" When we always try to portray others at their worst, what does this say about you?

---

365 WISDOM WHISPER ~ 111

" Words can build a nest or a cage; we can choose to comfort or control.

365 WISDOM WHISPER ~ 112

" Sometimes, when we fight fire with fire, the two can agree, and destruction can be avoided.

---

365 WISDOM WHISPER ~ 113

" If we are moving forward, it is impossible to direct our focus to what's behind us.

---

365 WISDOM WHISPER ~ 114

" The good in others can be blinded by our words of criticism.

365 WISDOM WHISPER ~ 115

"
Wisdom is known of her children, and she speaks without contention. Listen!

---

365 WISDOM WHISPER ~ 116

"
Bigotry and insensitivity are inseparable, and they are not easily disguised.

---

365 WISDOM WHISPER ~ 117

"
Hearts united in peace can ignite truth.

365 WISDOM WHISPER ~ 118

" Hate is not your friend; it only pretends to be when you are on its side.

---

365 WISDOM WHISPER ~ 119

" Hype is like fake gold. There is always somebody ready to make a quick sale. Buyer Beware!

---

365 WISDOM WHISPER ~ 120

" America's greatness is not in a mindset. Her greatness is in God.

365 WISDOM WHISPER ~ 121

" What we reveal to others outwardly may be totally different from who we are inwardly.

---

365 WISDOM WHISPER ~ 122

" The enemy always tries to deliver us his mail. Reply: Return to sender, address UNKNOWN.

---

365 WISDOM WHISPER ~ 123

" When many are shouting to be heard, maybe they are afraid that many are not listening.

365 WISDOM WHISPER ~ 124

"
It is not good to brag about the defeat of others, but it's noble to be a bridge of hope they can climb on.

---

365 WISDOM WHISPER ~ 125

"
Hate can abound because of constant injustice and seeks to avenge itself at any cost.

---

365 WISDOM WHISPER ~ 126

"
Beware of those who always know what's in your best interest, but it is a mute subject when it comes to them.

365 WISDOM WHISPER ~ 127

" If I stand up for what I believe in, is it wrong because you don't believe it?

---

365 WISDOM WHISPER ~ 128

" When we cast our pearls before swine, remember they can't appreciate pearls because they are swine.

---

365 WISDOM WHISPER ~ 129

" Many have lost their moral compass. I guess it wasn't working anyway because they deemed it antiquated.

365 WISDOM WHISPER ~ 130

" If sense is common, why are so many unfamiliar with it?

---

365 WISDOM WHISPER ~ 131

" When we speak words of hate, blame, ridicule, and discord against those with whom we disagree, don't forget if they disagree with us, they may feel justified in doing the same.

---

365 WISDOM WHISPER ~ 132

" When we try to find our significance in others, it is subject to change based on their approval.

365 WISDOM WHISPER ~ 133

"
Adam was asleep when God created a Womb-man (Eve). He had to be awake to see Increase!

---

365 WISDOM WHISPER ~ 134

"
Hypocrisy can stare us right in the face, but that doesn't mean we can see it.

---

365 WISDOM WHISPER ~ 135

"
The Accuser of the brethren spirit has captured many. Be careful of the fruit you eat and the seeds you sow. It could be the enemy's bait.

365 WISDOM WHISPER ~ 136

" Sometimes, people take our kindness for weakness because we allow it.

---

365 WISDOM WHISPER ~ 137

" Life can teach us a series of lessons, each with a test. Don't worry. It's an open book.

---

365 WISDOM WHISPER ~ 138

" Our character is not given; it is made, and our choices are part of the making process.

365 WISDOM WHISPER ~ 139

" An eagle's flight is not a path for small birds. He soars high towards the Sun!

---

365 WISDOM WHISPER ~ 140

" When we speak about the wrongs of others to make ourselves look good, the picture we are painting isn't a self-portrait but a duplicate.

---

365 WISDOM WHISPER ~ 141

" When we compromise ourselves in a relationship, it just might cause us to lose ourselves to gain something that wasn't ours in the first place.

365 WISDOM WHISPER ~ 142

" I refuse to allow statistics to govern my life, but I will allow every word that proceeds from the mouth of God to guide me.

---

365 WISDOM WHISPER ~ 143

" Stop wearing the hate. Love looks good on you.

---

365 WISDOM WHISPER ~ 144

" We don't need bars to be in a prison — only a defeated mindset.

365 WISDOM WHISPER ~ 145

"
    Our past mistakes may seem like a ball and chain, especially when we think there are no keys.

---

365 WISDOM WHISPER ~ 146

"
    Greatness is in you. Stop trying to find it in everyone else.

---

365 WISDOM WHISPER ~ 147

"
    I am a masterpiece. Stop trying to buy me because I am not for sale!

365 WISDOM WHISPER ~ 148

" If you lack understanding, get wisdom; she has all you need.

---

365 WISDOM WHISPER ~ 149

" When you treat yourself like a carbon copy, it might be hard for others to see you as the original.

---

365 WISDOM WHISPER ~ 150

" Propaganda is spread by those who have a heart for it and is received by those of the same.

365 WISDOM WHISPER ~ 151

" Sometimes, the truth brings pain, but its main objective is freedom.

---

365 WISDOM WHISPER ~ 152

" Maybe the train of injustice continues to run because many are ready to board.

---

365 WISDOM WHISPER ~ 153

" Sometimes, people will keep telling you all the things you want to hear because they have heard all the things that you have said.

365 WISDOM WHISPER ~ 154

"
Give honor to those to whom it is due. You never know the next time it could be you.

---

365 WISDOM WHISPER ~ 155

"
It is easy to walk in strife when we harbor offenses. It is easy to walk in love when we possess a pure heart.

---

365 WISDOM WHISPER ~ 156

"
When we allow the actions of some to make our hearts callous, we can miss the words of others that can allow our hearts to heal.

365 WISDOM WHISPER ~ 157

" Truth does not blind; deception does.

---

365 WISDOM WHISPER ~ 158

" When we arm ourselves with love, there is no reason to bear a grudge.

---

365 WISDOM WHISPER ~ 159

" Acts of kindness are seeds. All you sow, you shall reap.

365 WISDOM WHISPER ~ 160

" Being true to yourself is embracing who you are designed to be without feeling the need for apology or validation.

---

365 WISDOM WHISPER ~ 161

" Knowing peace within, we can command peace without!

---

365 WISDOM WHISPER ~ 162

" Motivation in the hearts of others may not captivate you as much as your own.

365 WISDOM WHISPER ~ 163

"
An insecure love has not embraced love as the cure. His love never fails.

_____

365 WISDOM WHISPER ~ 164

"
To so love responds by giving!

_____

365 WISDOM WHISPER ~ 165

"
When we strive to always make our presence known, some may find our absence timely.

365 WISDOM WHISPER ~ 166

"
People can think we are half-baked because they are not quite done.

---

365 WISDOM WHISPER ~ 167

"
Love can also be expressed in how we say No as well as how we say Yes.

---

365 WISDOM WHISPER ~ 168

"
We can be a slave to our past, and the chains that bind us could be our beliefs.

365 WISDOM WHISPER ~ 169

"
When we find our voice through silence, that which is golden can birth nations!

---

365 WISDOM WHISPER ~ 170

"
Everybody has a destination, but not all are called to be part of your journey.

---

365 WISDOM WHISPER ~ 171

"
Destination moves us forward, but doubts and fears can keep us in limbo.

365 WISDOM WHISPER ~ 172

" Big girls do cry, but our Father sees, hears, and responds.

---

365 WISDOM WHISPER ~ 173

" There is no magic in love, and its greatest secret is you!

---

365 WISDOM WHISPER ~ 174

" When we succumb to fear, we can allow faith to be silent.

365 WISDOM WHISPER ~ 175

"
Love has a sound; anyone can hear it when they are tuned in.

_____

365 WISDOM WHISPER ~ 176

"
Walls not only keep people out, but they also keep them in.

_____

365 WISDOM WHISPER ~ 177

"
If our response to hate is to keep silent, we have allowed hate to speak indefinitely!

365 WISDOM WHISPER ~ 178

" When you build a bridge that others can safely walk on, you become a part of their journey.

---

365 WISDOM WHISPER ~ 179

" Self-sabotage may not be easily recognized because we have become immune.

---

365 WISDOM WHISPER ~ 180

" Trips can be part of our journey. Stay Focused!

365 WISDOM WHISPER ~ 181

" Dreamers can be a part of our dreams, and they do not have to be nightmares.

---

365 WISDOM WHISPER ~ 182

" A gift we can give to others is honesty, but trust should never be packaged.

---

365 WISDOM WHISPER ~ 183

" When we invest in those we love, our return will yield priceless, valuable riches.

365 WISDOM WHISPER ~ 184

"   Hurt can make it hard for us to share and receive love, but love can make it possible to let go of the hurt.

---

365 WISDOM WHISPER ~ 185

"   Forgiveness is an act of our will, and patience is a virtue that can order its path.

---

365 WISDOM WHISPER ~ 186

"   The Bible was never meant just to be read. It was meant to be lived!

365 WISDOM WHISPER ~ 187

" Instead of stressing over the stress, I have decided to stress on the blessings!

---

365 WISDOM WHISPER ~ 188

" When we lead by example, it allows us to practice what we preach.

---

365 WISDOM WHISPER ~ 189

" When our words are quick to condemn, how can others truly hear?

365 WISDOM WHISPER ~ 190

" Grief is not a death sentence, for the joy of gladness is always prepared for a heart that mourns.

---

365 WISDOM WHISPER ~ 191

" When our fears are confirmed continuously by indoctrination, we all suffer the consequences. Blind Eyes See!

---

365 WISDOM WHISPER ~ 192

" Meekness is strength under control, and those who possess it don't mind if they appear weak to others. They know the power they wield.

365 WISDOM WHISPER ~ 193

" When the voices of others speak loudly to define you, don't listen because it's their definition, not yours.

---

365 WISDOM WHISPER ~ 194

" When we embrace our destiny, any stones thrown at us become stepping stones, not stumbling blocks.

---

365 WISDOM WHISPER ~ 195

" Don't throw in the towel but use it for a banner and wave it in a Victory Praise!

365 WISDOM WHISPER ~ 196

" Beloved, when I am reminded of who I am, I need not worry about who I was!

---

365 WISDOM WHISPER ~ 197

" We might not think that we are role models, but many lives we touch can bear the fruit.

---

365 WISDOM WHISPER ~ 198

" Don't take life for granted; we get to do this once.

365 WISDOM WHISPER ~ 199

" The words that we speak can be like painting on a canvas. The power to create is in our hands.

---

365 WISDOM WHISPER ~ 200

" May the walls of intolerance crumble to the mighty waters of Liberty!

---

365 WISDOM WHISPER ~ 201

" Fear invites us to run. Faith allows us to SPEAK!

365 WISDOM WHISPER ~ 202

" To smile at others costs us nothing, but to harbor hate is costly.

---

365 WISDOM WHISPER ~ 203

" Sometimes, a setback is a temporary landing pad for our launching.

---

365 WISDOM WHISPER ~ 204

" It's okay to be you; God designed you, and you are one of a kind.

365 WISDOM WHISPER ~ 205

"
The things others say about you can become real if you start to believe in them, whether good or bad.

_____

365 WISDOM WHISPER ~ 206

"
A heart that sees the good in others, is a heart that others can see the good in.

_____

365 WISDOM WHISPER ~ 207

"
Sometimes, we are on a road less traveled because it's divinely ordered of the Lord.

365 WISDOM WHISPER ~ 208

"   Many are not speaking into our lives because God has allowed them to be silent so that we can hear Him.

---

365 WISDOM WHISPER ~ 209

"   The challenges that we face are not meant to defeat us but to grow us up.

---

365 WISDOM WHISPER ~ 210

"   God is the Originator of our dreams. Seek Him for the interpretations.

365 WISDOM WHISPER ~ 211

"
Political propaganda is not God's sledgehammer. The Word of Truth is!

---

365 WISDOM WHISPER ~ 212

"
The same spirits attract not to oppose but to agree.

---

365 WISDOM WHISPER ~ 213

"
When we keep looking to others as our provision, we have lost sight of the reservoir inside of us.

365 WISDOM WHISPER ~ 214

" Many visual images we take in can cloud our judgment with intentions to infiltrate and control.

---

365 WISDOM WHISPER ~ 215

" A pebble thrown in a pond can make ripples; the rock in your mouth can move mountains!

---

365 WISDOM WHISPER ~ 216

" Love's resiliency can be seen in a heart that is not afraid to commit.

365 WISDOM WHISPER ~ 217

" When we constantly scrutinize others, we can become a spotlight.

---

365 WISDOM WHISPER ~ 218

" A heart that quickly accuses is a heart not acquainted with mercy.

---

365 WISDOM WHISPER ~ 219

" A rebellious spirit hates correction, but a contrite heart seeks for it.

365 WISDOM WHISPER ~ 220

"
Our God never forgets about the leftovers; they are remnants of the blessing!

---

365 WISDOM WHISPER ~ 221

"
Grey hairs are not always welcomed, but when they are persistent, we soon realize that silver is the new gold.

---

365 WISDOM WHISPER ~ 222

"
If our words are firing because we are trigger-happy, we have become an open target.

365 WISDOM WHISPER ~ 223

" Believing in what you choose to believe in should not discredit others.

---

365 WISDOM WHISPER ~ 224

" When men's hearts are set on evil, the opinions of right and wrong are not heard.

---

365 WISDOM WHISPER ~ 225

" Words can convey the condition of our hearts, for the heart contains them.

365 WISDOM WHISPER ~ 226

"
No matter how big it is, an ego can become prey to its pride.

---

365 WISDOM WHISPER ~ 227

"
To consistently shun wise counsel, we say yes to folly.

---

365 WISDOM WHISPER ~ 228

"
Anger and hatred can surely rob us.
They are like thieves who come to steal, especially when the door is left wide open.

365 WISDOM WHISPER ~ 229

" Constructive criticism is not ridicule or blame but correction bestowed in honor without shame.

---

365 WISDOM WHISPER ~ 230

" Surround yourself with those who can see your worth and not those who constantly talk about your wrongs.

---

365 WISDOM WHISPER ~ 231

" When we hold offenses, it can be like bearing a wound from a sharp knife. Wounds can heal, and so can a bleeding heart.

365 WISDOM WHISPER ~ 232

" It's hard for real people to be fake and for fake people to be real.

_____

365 WISDOM WHISPER ~ 233

" We all need that one friend who loves us regardless and doesn't mind correcting us when we are wrong.

_____

365 WISDOM WHISPER ~ 234

" Iron can only sharpen iron when there is contact.

365 WISDOM WHISPER ~ 235

" Challenges can test our abilities, but our abilities can be improved by our challenges.

---

365 WISDOM WHISPER ~ 236

" We are not responsible for the actions of others, but we are responsible for how we choose to respond.

---

365 WISDOM WHISPER ~ 237

" Hate and love are two powerful things; the one you choose to feed is the one that will grow.

365 WISDOM WHISPER ~ 238

" The roots of a tree can push through rocks, and much strength can be found in adversity.

---

365 WISDOM WHISPER ~ 239

" Each day is a Present that we get to receive and to give!

---

365 WISDOM WHISPER ~ 240

" Never judge a book by its cover; if we took the time to read it, some books would just be too complicated to understand.

365 WISDOM WHISPER ~ 241

" We need trust for trusting so that trust can be restored.

---

365 WISDOM WHISPER ~ 242

" Adversity can either rob us of our dreams or give us the inner strength to push us towards them.

---

365 WISDOM WHISPER ~ 243

" Love does not know how to hate, and hate does not know how to love.

365 WISDOM WHISPER ~ 244

"
Dreams occur when we are asleep. And dreams are fulfilled when we are awake.

---

365 WISDOM WHISPER ~ 245

"
Silence can't fix ignorance; the truth does.

---

365 WISDOM WHISPER ~ 246

"
Be careful of those who enjoy raining on other's parades. If they are marching with you, your parade could be next.

365 WISDOM WHISPER ~ 247

" The fragrance of betrayal can be stifling, but the aroma of forgiveness can refresh the soul!

---

365 WISDOM WHISPER ~ 248

" When we turn our regrets into gratitude, we can receive grace to grow.

---

365 WISDOM WHISPER ~ 249

" When we forget who we are, we can think that we are everything we are not.

365 WISDOM WHISPER ~ 250

"
Adversity can be a great teacher, but we are not always ready to learn.

---

365 WISDOM WHISPER ~ 251

"
If we run from fear, it will always chase us.

---

365 WISDOM WHISPER ~ 252

"
Unforgiveness can cause us to be chained to those we despise. Time to break free!

365 WISDOM WHISPER ~ 253

" We are not exempt from dishonesty shown towards us, especially if we have sown these seeds ourselves.

---

365 WISDOM WHISPER ~ 254

" Sometimes, when we feel we have nothing to lose, we can risk everything.

---

365 WISDOM WHISPER ~ 255

" The Bible becomes more than a book when we are intimate with the Author.

365 WISDOM WHISPER ~ 256

"
When we hide our pain, we can become chained to our hurt. His love sets the captive free!

---

365 WISDOM WHISPER ~ 257

"
When we try to always be like others, we will find it difficult to recognize who we really are.

---

365 WISDOM WHISPER ~ 258

"
Our endurance is developed in those things that allow us to press our way through.

365 WISDOM WHISPER ~ 259

" The crown of a king does not establish his character. His heart does.

---

365 WISDOM WHISPER ~ 260

" It is hard to get wisdom from the mouth of a fool because they can't digest it.

---

365 WISDOM WHISPER ~ 261

" True love never has a need to advertise, but pride loves to be seen.

365 WISDOM WHISPER ~ 262

" If the truth is always given to us sugarcoated, we might not develop a taste for it when it's not.

---

365 WISDOM WHISPER ~ 263

" A hammer can build and destroy, and so can your words.

---

365 WISDOM WHISPER ~ 264

" When looking for the forest and you can only see the trees, it's time to climb.

365 WISDOM WHISPER ~ 265

"
Beloved, when purpose speaks, destiny hears!

_____

365 WISDOM WHISPER ~ 266

"
People pleasers are not necessarily Peacemakers.

_____

365 WISDOM WHISPER ~ 267

"
The significance of love is seen in doing, and its impact can be profound once received.

365 WISDOM WHISPER ~ 268

"
There is a treasure in you, and we are usually unaware who God sends to open it up.

---

365 WISDOM WHISPER ~ 269

"
When you think it's too late to begin something new, don't let this be your excuse for not trying. Leap with faith!

---

365 WISDOM WHISPER ~ 270

"
Fake never becomes real, and real never becomes fake.

365 WISDOM WHISPER ~ 271

" Gifts are what we have been given; treasures are on the inside. Use them all!

---

365 WISDOM WHISPER ~ 272

" Self-affirmations can encourage our soul. Self-centeredness mars it.

---

365 WISDOM WHISPER ~ 273

" When we live our lives dancing to the tune of others, we might be too tired when our song starts playing.

365 WISDOM WHISPER ~ 274

" Defeat can be a springboard for those who choose to leap forward.

---

365 WISDOM WHISPER ~ 275

" A mirror gives us a reflection, but our heart is the true image of who we are.

---

365 WISDOM WHISPER ~ 276

" When we stop giving forgiveness, we can also stop receiving it.

365 WISDOM WHISPER ~ 277

" Staying in the past can put a hold on our present.

---

365 WISDOM WHISPER ~ 278

" When we invest in the world, we will surely lose our assets.

---

365 WISDOM WHISPER ~ 279

" Forgiveness is not always easy, but when we see ourselves as the main beneficiary, we can reap the benefits.

365 WISDOM WHISPER ~ 280

"
  Beloved, forgiveness is not arbitrary. It is mandatory!

_____

365 WISDOM WHISPER ~ 281

"
  To demonize other's points of view can bring scrutiny upon your own.

_____

365 WISDOM WHISPER ~ 282

"
  If we sit back waiting on chance, we could miss opportunity!

365 WISDOM WHISPER ~ 283

" Love is supposed to be exposed. It is a covering.

---

365 WISDOM WHISPER ~ 284

" The breath we breathe is a gift of life. Cherish it!

---

365 WISDOM WHISPER ~ 285

" If our attitude determines our altitude, it's time to check your gauges.

365 WISDOM WHISPER ~ 286

"" Some people choose to hate us without a cause, but we can choose to love them on purpose.

---

365 WISDOM WHISPER ~ 287

"" You will never climb out looking down. And you will never go forward looking back.

---

365 WISDOM WHISPER ~ 288

"" Beloved, we can't go broke when we owe others nothing but love.

365 WISDOM WHISPER ~ 289

" When someone tries to pass judgment on you, don't catch it.

---

365 WISDOM WHISPER ~ 290

" Fear is the currency of darkness, and faith is the currency of the Kingdom!

---

365 WISDOM WHISPER ~ 291

" It's okay to regret your past, but don't live there!

365 WISDOM WHISPER ~ 292

"
When we live our lives for others, we put ours on hold.

---

365 WISDOM WHISPER ~ 293

"
Our dreams aren't always contingent on our mountaintop experiences. Our valley experiences can also play an integral part.

---

365 WISDOM WHISPER ~ 294

"
Don't sit on transition; be a part of it.

365 WISDOM WHISPER ~ 295

" Mistakes can become successes when we try again.

---

365 WISDOM WHISPER ~ 296

" Don't abandon ship, for your cargo is too precious. Full steam ahead!

---

365 WISDOM WHISPER ~ 297

" The courage to be a winner comes with the first step.

365 WISDOM WHISPER ~ 298

"
Sometimes, being a shoulder for others to lean on, someone became that support for you.

---

365 WISDOM WHISPER ~ 299

"
Some people are on assignment to push us out of our nests, but fret not. This is by divine design!

---

365 WISDOM WHISPER ~ 300

"
Sometimes, we can be drawn to toxic people because of our poor resistance. Time to get inoculated with the Word!

365 WISDOM WHISPER ~ 301

"
   If we live in the minds of others, where and who are we when they stop thinking about us?

---

365 WISDOM WHISPER ~ 302

"
   Humanity isn't a blank canvas. We are divinely marked by the finger of the Almighty God!

---

365 WISDOM WHISPER ~ 303

"
   It is easy to sell ourselves out when we don't know that we have been bought with a great price!

365 WISDOM WHISPER ~ 304

"
Those who are desperate to be loved may easily find those who are willing to loan it.

---

365 WISDOM WHISPER ~ 305

"
Peace is a crown that reigns over circumstances!

---

365 WISDOM WHISPER ~ 306

"
Joseph started out as a dream chaser until he realized his dream chose him.

365 WISDOM WHISPER ~ 307

" When hate cripples us, we don't need crutches, only a clean heart.

---

365 WISDOM WHISPER ~ 308

" Beloved, remember that "self" can always have a best friend, and that friend is you.

---

365 WISDOM WHISPER ~ 309

" Love is always close because it's only a heart away.

365 WISDOM WHISPER ~ 310

"
Setbacks can be your setup to receive a miracle.

---

365 WISDOM WHISPER ~ 311

"
The Cross: Humanity's hope revealed and sealed!

---

365 WISDOM WHISPER ~ 312

"
Love is not only what we experience but also what we become.

365 WISDOM WHISPER ~ 313

"
Rogue comments can become fiery darts!

_____

365 WISDOM WHISPER ~ 314

"
Hate speaks a language all of its own, but so does love.

_____

365 WISDOM WHISPER ~ 315

"
When we wear our feelings on our sleeves, they can be easily manipulated.

365 WISDOM WHISPER ~ 316

" A surrendered life knows obedience.

---

365 WISDOM WHISPER ~ 317

" Sometimes, people treat us as slaves because we have made them our masters.

---

365 WISDOM WHISPER ~ 318

" Worship is like a sweet perfume; it saturates and consumes as we pour it out!

365 WISDOM WHISPER ~ 319

" It is difficult to hear love in words of ridicule, but truth spoken in love is more receptive.

---

365 WISDOM WHISPER ~ 320

" Hate is not capable of love, and love is not capable of hate.

---

365 WISDOM WHISPER ~ 321

" Faith is not blind it sees through the lens of hope and love.

365 WISDOM WHISPER ~ 322

"
    You cannot see yourself in a mirror in a dark place. Turn on the Light!

_____

365 WISDOM WHISPER ~ 323

"
    When we choose to forgive, we also choose to receive it.

_____

365 WISDOM WHISPER ~ 324

"
    Some people only want us for our goods, but they don't know our worth.

365 WISDOM WHISPER ~ 325

"
We don't fall for truth, we seek it. We don't seek for lies; we fall for them.

---

365 WISDOM WHISPER ~ 326

"
Many of us remain blind because we refuse to open our eyes.

---

365 WISDOM WHISPER ~ 327

"
God allowed darkness to exist because Light is its Master!

365 WISDOM WHISPER ~ 328

" The pride in us can remain dormant, or it can be made alive by the praises of others.

---

365 WISDOM WHISPER ~ 329

" A king's heart, blinded by ambition, cannot see that his way is marked.

---

365 WISDOM WHISPER ~ 330

" Encouraging words to a grieving heart is like a cooling rain on parched ground.

365 WISDOM WHISPER ~ 331

"
We are the Father's divine instruments, and He knows each tune.

---

365 WISDOM WHISPER ~ 332

"
Perfect love never binds, and its strength can never be broken!

---

365 WISDOM WHISPER ~ 333

"
When we live a life of transparency, Light can filter through it.

365 WISDOM WHISPER ~ 334

"
Our heart is a filter that allows the issues of life to flow. The word keeps the filter clean from impurities and contaminants.

---

365 WISDOM WHISPER ~ 335

"
Sometimes, God will cause us to be blinded by His light so we can be healed from our darkness.

---

365 WISDOM WHISPER ~ 336

"
When we speak the truth, many who hate the truth may seek its silence with lies.

365 WISDOM WHISPER ~ 337

" Love never forgets to love, but it always forgets to hate.

---

365 WISDOM WHISPER ~ 338

" How can we demand respect when we don't require it of ourselves?

---

365 WISDOM WHISPER ~ 339

" When we seek to hide from our hurt, it can be uncovered by our pain.

365 WISDOM WHISPER ~ 340

"
When we make someone else happy,
we will find that happiness can be shared.

---

365 WISDOM WHISPER ~ 341

"
When our hurt is masked by hate, hurt
can become silent, allowing hate to be the
only voice to speak.

---

365 WISDOM WHISPER ~ 342

"
Puppets need strings, and those who
control the strings need the puppets.

365 WISDOM WHISPER ~ 343

" Sometimes, we have to lose a lot to gain what truly matters.

---

365 WISDOM WHISPER ~ 344

" A heart that will forgive can find forgiveness in forgiving.

---

365 WISDOM WHISPER ~ 345

" Love has no race but only hearts united as One!

365 WISDOM WHISPER ~ 346

" Many are afraid to love because they have been hurt, and many are hurting to be loved.

---

365 WISDOM WHISPER ~ 347

" We don't wake up to forsake truth. We wake up to follow after it.

---

365 WISDOM WHISPER ~ 348

" A proud look reveals a heart that is clueless of its poison.

365 WISDOM WHISPER ~ 349

" Those things that are not spoken can be the very things that are heard the loudest.

---

365 WISDOM WHISPER ~ 350

" Instead of faking it until you make it, Faith It!

---

365 WISDOM WHISPER ~ 351

" If we see our happiness in others, we will keep chasing after them to receive it.

365 WISDOM WHISPER ~ 352

"
When the Light wakes us up, it's hard to go back to sleep.

---

365 WISDOM WHISPER ~ 353

"
Evil can't win, but it is hoping that we believe by fear that it can.

---

365 WISDOM WHISPER ~ 354

"
The words we speak can reveal our heart, but we are often too deaf to hear them.

365 WISDOM WHISPER ~ 355

" Sin can offer us an escape, but its purpose is to keep us lost.

---

365 WISDOM WHISPER ~ 356

" We can be easily manipulated by our hurt and remain its victim.

---

365 WISDOM WHISPER ~ 357

" If praise is your lifestyle, it will change your style of life radically!

365 WISDOM WHISPER ~ 358

" Love is never wasted on hate because hate is always desperate for love.

_____

365 WISDOM WHISPER ~ 359

" I once was in love with love, until I came to realize, love is more than a four-letter word.

_____

365 WISDOM WHISPER ~ 360

" The answer to hate is you, and the answer to love is you!

365 WISDOM WHISPER ~ 361

" Our tomorrows can't rewrite our destiny, but they can reveal its path.

---

365 WISDOM WHISPER ~ 362

" A flower doesn't decide to bloom but yields to the process!

---

365 WISDOM WHISPER ~ 363

" Ignorance is a blindfold many choose to wear, even if they are afforded the opportunity not to.

365 WISDOM WHISPER ~ 364

" Greed is always hungry and seeks a belly to fill.

---

365 WISDOM WHISPER ~ 365

" An unforgiving heart might not recognize its own hate because of blindness.

- ABOUT THE AUTHOR -

Amanda Nabors is a multifaceted professional with a diverse range of talents and a strong spiritual calling. As an educator, she dedicates herself to nurturing and guiding young minds, imparting knowledge with a blend of patience and enthusiasm. Her passion for writing and poetry allows her to express her thoughts and emotions creatively, often exploring profound themes and personal experiences.

In addition to her literary pursuits, Amanda is also a skilled artist and songwriter, where she combines her artistic vision with melodious elements to craft unique and meaningful compositions. Her role as an ordained minister, intercessor, and motivational speaker highlights her ability to inspire and uplift others, drawing on her own life experiences and insights to encourage positive change and personal growth.